THE NO NONSENSE KEY

Read *Understanding Estate Planning and Wills*

- If you want to provide for the future security of your loved ones
- If you want to learn about wills, trusts, and probate
- If you want to understand the best ways of limiting estate taxes
- If you want to know what common mistakes to avoid

THE NO NONSENSE LIBRARY

NO NONSENSE LEGAL GUIDES

Understanding Estate Planning and Wills, Revised Edition
How to Choose A Lawyer

NO NONSENSE FINANCIAL GUIDES

How to Finance Your Child's College Education, Revised Edition
How to Use Credit and Credit Cards, Revised Edition
Understanding Treasury Bills and Other U.S. Government Securities,
  Revised Edition
Understanding Tax-Exempt Bonds
Understanding Money Market Funds, Revised Edition
Understanding Mutual Funds, Revised Edition
Understanding IRAs, Revised Edition
Understanding Common Stocks, Revised Edition
Understanding the Stock Market, Revised Edition
Understanding Stock Options and Futures Markets, Revised Edition
How to Choose a Discount Stockbroker, Revised Edition
How to Make Personal Financial Planning Work for You
How to Plan and Invest for Your Retirement
The New Tax Law and What It Means to You

NO NONSENSE REAL ESTATE GUIDES

Understanding Condominiums and Co-ops, Revised Edition
Understanding Buying and Selling a House, Revised Edition
Understanding Mortgages and Home Equity Loans, Revised Edition
Refinancing Your Mortgage, Revised Edition

OTHER NO NONSENSE GUIDES

Car Guides
Career Guides
Cooking Guides
Health Guides
Parenting Guides
Photography Guides
Study Guides
Success Guides
Wine Guides

NO-NONSENSE LEGAL GUIDE

UNDERSTANDING ESTATE PLANNING AND WILLS

REVISED EDITION

Stephen H. Green and
Phyllis C. Kaufman

LONGMEADOW PRESS

To Moose and Princess

Understanding Estate Planning and Wills, Revised Edition

Copyright © 1985, 1987 by Arnold Corrigan and Phyllis C. Kaufman. All rights reserved.

Design by Adrian Taylor.
Production services by William S. Konecky Associates, New York.

ISBN: 0-681-40252-0

Printed in the United States of America

0 9 8 7 6 5 4 3

To Moose and Princess

CONTENTS

PREFACE

There is no substitute for the security and contentment of knowing that your loved ones will be taken care of. But how can you provide for the future of those you love? How can you be sure that everything you have worked so hard for will benefit those you care about most?

The only way is to plan your estate—to take the time now to make decisions for the future.

The No-Nonsense Guide, *Understanding Estate Planning and Wills* will acquaint you with wills, trusts, and probate. You will learn what to do and what mistakes to avoid. You will learn ways of limiting estate taxes.

You will learn how good and thoughtful estate planning can bring you peace and contentment.

PART I
INTRODUCTION

1

WHAT IS ESTATE PLANNING?

Estate planning is providing for the future. It is the process by which you think about and decide how to distribute your property and possessions ("estate") to loved ones and friends and then adopt a plan of action designed to achieve these goals while, at the same time, saving the most in taxes.

How your estate is handled—in terms of efficiency, economy, competence and sensitivity—is also important. It involves much more than just "making a will," although that is certainly part of the process.

One very important result of estate planning is the psychological relief you feel after you have completed the procedure. Knowing that your plan has been carefully considered, and that all the necessary documents have been properly prepared to carry out your wishes, is a great comfort.

Another important purpose of estate planning is to provide a clear "roadmap" for handling your estate when the time comes. A good plan will ease the problems of administration, eliminate arguments and, hopefully, save taxes, so that your beneficiaries will enjoy more of what you want them to receive.

Periodic Review

Estate planning is not a once-in-a-lifetime proposition. Family relationships change. Personal desires change. Individual finances change. The tax laws change. Each factor must be considered. It is a good idea to review your estate plan at least every three years, and whenever there is a meaningful change in the size of your estate or your personal situation.

Questions to Ask

A substantial portion of the estate planning process involves asking yourself a lot of questions. These include:

- What are your assets?
- How are they owned? (Individually, or jointly with a spouse or other person?)
- Where do you want them to go when you die?
- Do you have other assets over which you have control?
- Do you have a pension or other retirement benefits coming due?
- Is there a business interest to think about?
- What if your spouse remarries soon after you die?
- Are your children or grandchildren old enough, or mature enough, to handle any assets you may want to give them?
- Are there special people outside your immediate family whom you want to remember?
- Do you want to leave anything to charity?
- Who will be the person you name to be sure that your wishes are carried out?
- Can what you want to do be overturned by, for example, people not named to inherit your property, or by people who think they did not receive enough?

As we go through the estate planning process, you will learn how your answers to these questions affect your plan.

Conclusion

Remember that the value of a will is directly proportionate to the quality of the planning which preceded it.

If you walk into a lawyer's office and walk out with a will for $25, you probably got your money's worth.

4

You probably also got a will similar to (if not exactly the same as) the will of every other client of that office who walked out with a $25 will. That inexpensive will may or may not accomplish what you want and need. It may or may not facilitate administration of your estate when the time comes. It may or may not save taxes and administration expenses. Why leave so much open to doubt?

2

PROFESSIONAL ASSISTANCE

Estate planning is too important and complex to be left to chance. Laws governing estates are intricate and vary from state to state. Tax laws are constantly changing. And when problems arise, you won't be around to solve them.

It is for these and many other reasons that we urge you to seek professional assistance. Take the time to assemble a "team" to work with, a team of people you can talk to and trust.

Legal Advice

While you are the captain of your team, a competent estate lawyer is definitely your quarterback. Remember that attorneys, more and more, are specializing, and the lawyer you trust and admire for his or her courtroom skills might not be the best choice for your estate planning. Your business lawyer will be on the team, giving advice and recommendations on business affairs, but your estate lawyer should be someone who has significant experience, and is current, in that area.

Finding the Right Lawyer

How do you find the right lawyer? There are many ways. First, ask your own attorney for a recommendation. Ask your relatives and friends. The best recommendation is from someone who has had a favorable experience with a good lawyer. If you are not satisfied with the references you receive, go to the local bar association. It should have a list of attorneys who specialize in estate planning.

Take the names of several attorneys and interview them. Ask as many questions as you like. Make sure that you ask about fees (both for the interview and for any work that may be done later). Ask if he/she charges on an hourly or a flat-rate basis. If it is hourly, ask for an estimate of the number of hours he/she anticipates spending on your case. Understand that this is just an estimate and that unforeseen complications could increase the fee.

If the attorney is a member of a firm, ask who will be doing the actual work on your case. Will it be the person you are interviewing, or a junior associate?

Are you comfortable with the answers you receive? Do not engage an attorney until you find one you have confidence in and trust. Then ask him/her to give you a letter describing what services will be performed and what you will be charged. (For more information, see the No-Nonsense Legal Guide, *How to Choose a Lawyer*.)

Other Team Members

Your accountant should also play a significant role in your estate planning, as will your banker, stockbroker, investment adviser, insurance agent, and quite possibly your priest, minister or rabbi. They can provide important information and advice on both the legal and personal decisions you will make.

3

WHO'S WHO

The rules and customs surrounding the passing of property and belongings have been evolving for centuries. Most American laws reflect our English legal heritage, and the terms which apply to estates originated there.

Estate

Your "estate" is the sum total of all your assets, including real property, cash, stocks, bonds, furniture, jewelry, memorabilia, insurance, and rights and claims under employee benefit plans, trusts and other estates. (See the *No-Nonsense Estate Planning Information Summary* in Appendix A.)

Estate Planning

"Estate Planning" is the act of deciding who will receive each item that you own and on what terms, after you die, and preparing to effect those decisions.

Beneficiary

A beneficiary is a person who is designated by you, in your will, to share in your estate.

Heir

An heir is a person who the law states will, because of his/her relationship to you, receive items from your estate, if you should die without a valid will. The term is sometimes used synonymously with "beneficiary."

Executor

An executor is a person or entity (such as a bank) named in your will to administer your estate. This means paying your liabilities, administration expenses, and estate and inheritance taxes, and distributing the assets of your estate according to the terms and conditions of your will, and in accordance with law.

Administrator

An administrator is a person appointed by the court to administer your estate, when the named executor cannot or will not perform, when no executor has been named, or when there is no will.

Fiduciary

A fiduciary is any person in a position of trust. Executors and administrators are fiduciaries; so are trustees and guardians.

4

CAN WE TALK?

The disposition of assets by will may cause family arguments and dissension. A substantial portion of these problems can be avoided if, before or after you execute your will, you take the time to sit with your family (and your friends, if they are included in your generosity) and tell them what you plan to do and why.

This isn't an easy thing to do. However, when you think that it might avoid many problems for those you love, at a time when they will need all the help they can get, you will be able to do it.

If you like, you can tell everybody all of the details in your will. But that really isn't necessary. You might choose to tell them that you have prepared a will and that you have given a copy of it to a specific individual, your lawyer, for example, for safekeeping.

You needn't go into each and every detail of disposition. You may want to tell them in general terms that you have given careful consideration to the needs, desires and special situations of each individual. You may want to indicate that certain people may receive bequests larger or smaller than others, and that most of all, you hope there will be no arguments about what you have done.

PART II
WILLS

5

WHAT IS A WILL?

A will is usually the cornerstone of an estate plan. It is the legal document which states how you want to dispose of your property and personal belongings after you die. It also states who you want to take charge of carrying out your wishes. You must be of "sound mind" when you write it and it must conform to certain legal requirements, which vary from state to state.

Witnesses

All wills must be signed and dated, and they should be witnessed to make their processing easier. The laws of your state will determine whether your signature is required on every page or just at the end, and who can or cannot be a witness.

In general, a certain minimum number of witnesses who know who you are must also sign your will. The number of witnesses required and who may be a witness varies among the states.

Self-proving Wills

In some states, wills may be "self-proving," which means that if the witnesses also sign the will in the presence of a notary, they will not have to appear to validate their signatures when the will is submitted for probate. (See Chapter 17.)

This may seem to be a small detail, but it can be important, especially if the witnesses can't be found, or it is inconvenient for them to come to the courthouse. Remember that neighbors move away, your lawyer's secretary may leave his/her employ, or your witnesses may die before you do.

Holographic Will

A "holographic" will is one which is entirely handwritten by the person whose will it is. Most states will accept holographic wills for probate, but they can cause a lot of problems.

There was, not long ago, a situation where a bedridden gentleman wrote his "will" on the wall above his bed. No other will was found, and the portion of the wall on which the "will" was written was cut out and brought to the probate office. After it was initially accepted, it was challenged by dissatisfied heirs. It withstood the challenge, but the court battle was very costly.

Problems of Holographic Wills

The principal problem with a holographic will is that it usually does not involve the reasoned planning which should precede the preparation of a will. It may omit important provisions. A search may have to be done to be sure that there is no later will. Witnesses (perhaps paid "experts") may have to be brought in to court to verify the fact that the writing and the signature are yours. And because a holographic will is not usually prepared with legal assistance, it may be ambiguous, try to do things that cannot be easily done, and result in a costly battle between beneficiaries. Finally, the costs of administering an estate subject to a holographic will will likely be higher than the costs of administering an estate which is subject to a well-prepared will.

If the holographic will is so confusing, disorganized, or unclear that it prolongs estate administration, and increases aggravation and cost, it is possible that everyone would have been better off if there had been no such will. See Chapter 16.

6

WILLS WITH PERSONALITY

Creative Wills

A will is a serious document. It disposes of your assets and involves intense planning for the benefit of your loved ones.

It may also be a creative document. You can say things in your will that you want people to know. You can tell them how much you love them. You can explain why you have done the things you did. You can express your hopes for the future. So long as it otherwise meets legal requirements, your will can be a vehicle for personal expression. A word of advice: Don't say nasty things about people; that could lead to libel suits against your estate.

Videotape Wills

In some states your "will" could be a videotape of you saying what you want to happen. This could be a more personalized way of expressing your wishes. But you must be *very sure* that such wills are valid in your state, and you must also be sure not to leave out the important provisions which would appear in a written document. If there is any doubt, a written will is best. A videotape could accompany your written will, as a "last message" to your family, to be treasured, like a photograph.

7

GENERAL PROVISIONS THAT SHOULD BE INCLUDED IN YOUR WILL

This chapter will summarize some important provisions that should be included in your will. Subsequent chapters will deal with a number of these items in more detail.

Laws

Your will should comply with all applicable provisions of state law. Professional assistance will assure compliance.

All Assets

Your will should dispose of all your assets. This includes real estate, cash, stocks, bonds and other property, both tangible and intangible, as well as special items of sentimental value.

Beneficiaries

You must decide who are the people to whom you want to leave property or money. They will probably include family and friends, but may also include charities, your church or synagogue, or even your dog or cat. (See Chapter 10.)

Executors and Trustees

Your executors and trustees (called "fiduciaries") and their successors must be clearly identified and their

16

powers must be specified so that they can act without difficulty or delay in administering your estate. (See Chapter 11.)

Taxes

You must consider the state and federal tax consequences of your bequests and the effect of taxes on your estate. (See Chapters 19 and 20.)

Guardian

If minor children are involved, your will should appoint a guardian or guardians for them, and successor guardian(s) in case the original appointees cannot serve. (See Chapter 11.)

Real Estate

You must decide who will receive any real estate you own, keeping in mind that joint ownership of real estate may take the property out of your estate entirely for probate purposes. Remember that if you own a house with your spouse, you will probably be either tenants by the entireties (that is, joint owners because of marriage) or joint tenants. You could also own property jointly with someone else. In either of these cases, the property would not be yours to bequeath if your joint owner survives you, because the property will, by law, pass to and be solely owned by him/her. (See Chapter 9.)

Another form of ownership is "tenancy in common," which means that you own a portion of the property with another person, or other people; you can dispose of your ownership portion (usually a fractional interest) in your will.

Intangible Property

You must decide what to do with intangible property. Intangible property includes cash, stocks, bonds, bank accounts, pension benefits and other similar property which is not "physical."

17

Tangible Property

Tangible property includes household furnishings, automobiles, jewelry, collectibles, and other "physical" assets.

Cash Bequests

If you are going to make cash bequests, you must be sure that, after all the taxes, expenses and administration costs are paid, there is enough cash available to actually pay them. One source of cash can come from the sale of other assets, provided that you have not specifically given them to someone else in your will.

Residue

What remains in your estate after all debts, expenses and taxes are paid, and all specific bequests are given out, is called the "residue." The disposition of the residue is in accordance with the provisions you put in the "residuary clause" in your will. This clause should specifically cover who is to receive the residue and on what terms.

You must name a residuary beneficiary(s) and you ought also to name a successor to him/her, in case the residuary beneficiary predeceases you.

8

TANGIBLE PERSONAL PROPERTY

Families are often torn apart by battles over who should get the milkglass vase or the spinning wheel. The dollar value may be immaterial, but people have been known to stop speaking because of arguments over the monogrammed shot glasses or the coconut face brought back from Florida 30 years ago.

The best way to avoid these problems is to *specifically* identify items of tangible personal property and who is to receive them. If such specific identification is included in the will, the executor must give the items to the people named. If there is unhappiness about who got what, only you can be blamed; at least the people who survive need not argue with each other, since you made the decision.

Memorandum

Often a person includes in a will a statement that he or she will leave a list or memorandum, stating who is to receive specified items of tangible personal property. That may be fine, if the list can be found and everyone agrees to honor it. But since it is not in the will, it isn't binding on your executor or beneficiaries. That means that there can still be arguments, and the executor is caught in the middle. Even worse, if the executor is one of the beneficiaries, the possibilities for bitter argument and litigation are enhanced.

Keep in mind that, unless you make other provision in your will, a person who receives such property (or any asset for that matter) may be obligated to pay the estate and/or inheritance tax on its value. You could, however, provide that the taxes are to be paid out of the residue of your estate.

19

9

REAL ESTATE

Often, but not always, real estate is owned jointly, with spouses or others. If that is the case, it will automatically pass to the survivor, and will not be governed by the terms of your will. On the death of the survivor, the property will be governed by his/her will.

Three Suggestions

Assuming that the real estate is *not* owned jointly, your will should provide for its disposition, and there are *at least* three ways to handle it. The first is to order the executor to sell the property and either distribute the proceeds to named persons, or add the proceeds to the residue of your estate.

Another is to leave the property outright to a named person, persons, or entity(s). This will raise questions about who pays the estate or inheritance tax with respect to the property. You should be confident that the named beneficiary is able to handle the financial and other responsibilities of owning real estate.

A third way to dispose of real estate is to leave it to a person for use during his or her lifetime (called a "life estate"), and provide that on the death of that person, the property passes outright to another person, persons, or entity(s). This enables a person who has been living in or using the property to remain for his or her lifetime, but conveys no ownership rights. It is often used to ensure that a spouse or parent will be able to live in the family house for the rest of his/her lifetime.

If you choose the last alternative, you must state

who will be responsible for the property's expenses and maintenance during the life of the life tenant. You should also think about whether the ultimate beneficiary will be too old to enjoy it when he/she eventually gets the property. Language in the will must be very carefully and specifically drafted if a life estate is used.

10

BENEFICIARIES

A beneficiary is any person or entity that you designate to receive a share of your estate. You can name as a beneficiary almost any person or entity you choose. In some states, with various restrictions and requirements, you can even name animals as your beneficiaries. Your freedom of selection is almost total and the beneficiaries should be clearly identified.

But tax laws and state probate laws may, or should, affect your choices.

Think First

You may want to leave everything outright to your spouse. But that may not be the best way to do it for tax reasons. Consider that if your spouse dies soon after you, or before he/she has had a chance to use a substantial portion of your estate, the remainder of your assets will then become fully taxable as part of his/her estate. This is especially not a good way to proceed if your combined assets exceed the federal estate tax minimums of $500,000 in 1986 and $600,000 in 1987 and thereafter. See Chapter 19 for more detailed federal tax discussion.

Spouse

Taxes aside, how do state laws affect the naming of beneficiaries? In most states, unless you have a binding and legal contract to the contrary (for example a prenuptial agreement), you ordinarily may not cut your spouse out of your estate. In fact, in some states, he/she may be entitled to one-half, or one-third, or some other portion of your estate no matter *what* your wishes are.

Children

In most states, children do not enjoy the same legal right to share in an estate as does a spouse. So long as it is clear that you knowingly and intentionally did not name a child or children as beneficiary(s), they probably can't make a claim against your estate. Your state's laws should be examined to see what can and cannot be done.

Adopted or "Illegitimate" Children

In some states, adopted or "illegitimate" children have no legal right to inherit from their adoptive or natural parents, respectively. Merely using the term "children," or "issue" (an English legal term for children, grandchildren, etc.) in your will may not be adequate to provide for them unless you make specific reference to them.

On the other hand, some states assume that adopted and/or illegitimate children *are* to be considered and treated just as your other children are. So if you intend to *exclude* them from sharing in your estate, you should be specific in your will.

If you want to *include* adopted and illegitimate children in your estate, it is a good idea to refer to them specifically. For example, you could say, "I give to my children, Lydia Marx and Joshua Dingle. . . ." Or, you could include them by specific reference, such as "I give to my children, both adopted and those of which I am the natural parent. . . ."

Additional children might be born after you execute your will, or after you die. If that is possible, you ought to include a provision in your will stating that all children whenever born of whom you are the parent shall be treated as your children for all purposes in your will.

While a child may not have a legal right to inherit from a parent's estate in your state, it is possible that the parent of your child (in either a divorce or illegitimacy situation) may have a claim against you and your estate for the support of that child. That may not seem to make sense, but it is possible that it could happen. If there is such a possibility, and you have any concern about it, you should consult your attorney. Be sure to be completely candid about the situation.

Other Possible Beneficiaries

There are, of course, other alternative beneficiaries such as friends, neighbors, co-workers, employees, charities, trusts (see Chapter 23), organizations or governmental bodies. There are virtually *no restrictions* on what you can do. But remember that what you do is subject to the possible rights of others under the laws of your state.

Contingent Beneficiaries

You should be sure, also, to provide for "contingent" beneficiaries, in case the people or entities you name as beneficiaries aren't in existence either when you die or when your executor is ready to make distributions.

For example, what happens if you leave $1,000 to Finian, but Finian dies before you do? The bequest to him may "lapse," which means that his $1,000 goes into the residue of your estate and passes to whomever you name as your residuary beneficiary. Or, the laws of some states may provide that Finian's children will receive what he would have been entitled to. What if Finian dies 30 days after you do, but before your executor was able to pay his bequest to him? In that case, the $1,000 would be paid to *his* estate, and will in turn pass to whomever *he* names as his beneficiaries or, if he had no will, to the persons who inherit under the laws of his state.

You can provide that someone must survive you, or survive you by a certain number of days, to be entitled to a bequest. And you can also provide that if he/she doesn't, then his/her bequest will pass to another named beneficiary or revert to the residue of your estate. The choices are yours.

What If All Your Bequests Fail?

If all of your bequests fail because your beneficiaries do not survive you, or don't survive you for a specified period of time, and you make no provision for contingent beneficiaries, your estate will be distributed in accordance with the law of your state as though you had no will at all. That means, for example, that if you are not survived by spouse, parents, grandparents, children, sisters or brothers, your estate could pass to your nieces or nephews or cousins you may have never seen or never liked. And if you have no relatives whatsoever, your estate may even pass to your state—an extreme and unlikely possibility, but still a possibility.

Conclusion

In considering what to do and say in your will you should take the time and try to cover as many "what ifs" as possible, none more important than in the area of beneficiaries.

11

FIDUCIARIES

A fiduciary is a person who is put in a position of trust and who must act solely in the best interest of the person or persons who are the beneficiaries of that trust. A fiduciary can be a natural person or an entity authorized under state law to act in such a capacity (such as a bank or trust company). Those who are appointed as executors, administrators, trustees and guardians are all fiduciaries.

Qualities of a Fiduciary

Careful thought must be given to naming the fiduciaries who will carry out the plan embodied in your will. The person(s) you name should be trustworthy, responsible, attentive to details and filing requirements and sensitive to your family situation. They can be friends, relatives, neighbors or persons with whom you have had professional contact (lawyers and accountants, for example), or legally acceptable institutions. And you can certainly name more than one person or entity, or a combination of both.

Successor Fiduciary(s)

Once you have done the serious thinking and have named as fiduciaries people or institutions in whom you have confidence, you really ought to consider who you would want to serve if those you named did not, or could not, serve. The successor fiduciary(s) should meet all of the same tests you imposed in naming the initial designees.

Duties of an Executor or Administrator

The duties of the person appointed as your executor (or appointed by the court or probate authority as your administrator) will include filing your will for probate, collecting all of your probate assets, paying your outstanding bills and administration expenses, filing the appropriate federal and state income tax returns (both for the estate and for your "final life period," as may be necessary), filing the required estate and inheritance tax returns, making the appropriate filings with the local probate authorities, and eventually distributing the assets of your estate in accordance with the instructions in your will.

Duties of a Trustee

You will have a trustee if you use a trust in your will or in your lifetime. Your trustee carries out the terms of the trust document under which he/she/it is appointed, collecting income, paying expenses, making distributions, filing the appropriate tax returns and reports to beneficiaries, and accounting for all of his/her/its actions by way of official court filings or informal accountings and agreements with the trust beneficiaries.

Powers

Once you have carefully and thoughtfully chosen your fiduciaries, you don't want to tie their hands. If you don't describe the powers your fiduciaries are to have, they will be limited to acting in accordance with the fiduciary laws of your state.

For example, unless you grant specific investment powers, your fiduciaries will be limited to certain types of investments allowed under the fiduciary law. It may be necessary for them to obtain special permission from the appropriate court if they want to take actions not otherwise authorized in the powers you give them.

Give Specific and Broad Powers

For example, the fiduciary laws may limit estate or trust investments to utility stocks (electric company, phone company, and the like), or to AAA-rated corporate or municipal bonds. That means your executor or trustee might not be able to invest in other top-quality securities, or worse, may be required to sell those which do not meet the statutory tests. Such a sale may not only be contrary to your expectations, it may also result in adverse tax consequences.

A further example: If your fiduciary wants to sell real estate, unless you make clear in the fiduciary powers provision that he/she/it may do so, it will probably be necessary to obtain court approval for such a sale. That involves delay, possibly more lawyer's fees, court fees and bonding fees. All of that aggravation and expense can be avoided simply by empowering the fiduciary to sell real estate. The same considerations may apply to settling claims against the estate; absent the specific power to do so, court approval may be necessary, at the expense of greater cost and delay.

You might be wondering why you would *want* to give your fiduciary such broad powers that he/she/it might take actions that could be unwise. If that is a genuine concern, then the powers should not be so broad. But that says something about the degree of trust you have in your fiduciary, and perhaps greater thought should be given to whom you name.

Standard of Care

All fiduciaries are held to a high standard of care and integrity. Unless you specifically said that they could, for example, your fiduciaries could not invest your money in speculative Antarctic gold mine stocks. They must act to protect the security of the assets over which they have control and, unless otherwise directed in your will, they must seek to generate reasonable income. If they are not honest, or do not act with a high degree of care, they may be removed, or "surcharged" (a kind of penalty for loss), or otherwise held accountable for loss or damage to the estate or trust.

Fees

Fiduciaries are entitled to fees for what they do. Often such fees are based on the size of the estate, the "principal" assets of the trust and/or the income of the trust. Banks will ordinarily tell you what their fees are in prepared schedules, but such fees are subject to change as time passes. For individual fiduciaries, there are no "published" fee schedules. But local inheritance tax authorities and courts which have jurisdiction over estates and trusts control the allowance of fees, and may even tell you in advance what they use as guidelines in determining allowable charges. You can negotiate fees, and you can specify in your will or trust document what fees may be charged. If you choose to specify such fees in the document(s), you should obtain the advance agreement of the fiduciary whom you are seeking to bind in such a way; otherwise, such a provision may not be enforceable.

Banks as Fiduciaries

Banks are accustomed and legally authorized to act as fiduciaries, and most are set up to do so on a routine basis. They may act as sole fiduciary, or as co-fiduciary with specific individual(s) you name in your will or trust. Some banks will agree to act solely on a fee-for-service basis, so that even if they are not named as fiduciary, or co-fiduciary, they will handle the record-keeping, reporting and filing requirements for your estate. That is something you and your lawyer ought to consider.

The Choice Is Yours

Beware of lawyers who tell you that fiduciaries *must* be lawyers. This is completely untrue. And beware of lawyers who name themselves as your fiduciaries without you telling them to do so. You have freedom of choice. You also have a duty to read carefully what you are asked to sign. Be sure that the person who prepares your will doesn't sneak him/herself in there without your knowledge.

Why would someone try to become a fiduciary? Very simply because executors, trustees and guardians are or may be entitled to be paid (and sometimes handsomely) for their services.

Guardian(s) for Minor Children

If you have minor children, you should provide for the appointment of a guardian, or guardians, should your spouse (or their other parent, if your current spouse is not their parent) not survive you. If you do not so provide, you will be turning over to a court the decision as to who should be entrusted with the responsibility for the care of your minor children. In addition to all the uncertainty and trauma that can involve, it can also be a costly process—whatever it costs your estate to do that, it means that fewer assets will be available for your children. The continuing cost can be high, too, since the court may require that periodic reports be filed by its appointed guardian.

Who Should Be a Guardian?

That process can in most, if not all, states be avoided by the designation of guardian(s) in your will. The person, or persons, named should be people known to you and your children. They should also be people whom you can trust to make life decisions for your chidren (where to live, where to go to school, medical care decisions).

Get Their Consent

Before you name anyone in your will, however, you should be sure to speak with him/her/them and obtain his/her/their consent. The responsibility, and the possible lifestyle adjustments which may be required, are too significant for surprises. The person(s) named should be aware of what may be involved, and willing to take on the task.

Successor Guardians

It is also a good idea to name successor, or contingent, guardians, if it should happen that the people you designate are, when the time comes, unable or unwilling to assume the responsibility. Remember that people's circumstances change (they divorce, they die, they lose jobs or become ill), and unless you keep your will up-to-date, you may find that your original choice is no longer a realistic one.

12

OTHER IMPORTANT CLAUSES

Payment of Expenses

Your will should provide for the payment of your outstanding debts, expenses of your last illness, funeral and related burial expenses. If you do not so provide, it is possible in some states that your spouse and/or children could be liable for some if not all of such expenses. Also, by being specific, you eliminate possible arguments over who should be responsible for such payments.

Tax Clauses

Your will ought to provide that where a fiduciary can take certain deductions against income tax or estate tax, he/she/it should have the right to do what is most favorable to your beneficiaries and your estate. Skilled counseling is needed in order to determine what course of action is most beneficial. A provision permitting the fiduciary to elect alternatives is important. And keep in mind that the ability to do adequate post-mortem tax planning may depend not only on what is in your will, but also on how you fulfill your lifetime estate and financial planning responsibilities.

Who Pays the Taxes?

Another important tax clause which should not be overlooked is the one which says who should bear the tax on the bequests in your will. For example, if you give specific bequests of money or property to Kerry

Smith or Mark Jones and give the rest of your estate to your spouse, you should say whether Kerry and Mark must pay the estate and inheritance taxes on what they receive, or whether all such taxes are to be paid from the residue of your estate, which in this case means what your spouse will receive. If the latter option is what you choose, then your spouse will actually pay the taxes on Kerry and Mark's bequests. The failure to say anything could, depending on the probate laws of your state, create a result you didn't expect or desire.

Spendthrift Clause

There are in this world people who go around buying interests in estates, and there are people who try to sell or borrow against their interests in estates. In addition, in some states, a person's interest in an estate may be subject to the claims of creditors. Once a person's bequest is paid to him/her, of course, it is beyond the control of any will or fiduciary to affect what happens. But before the bequest is paid, proper language in a will or trust can prevent the estate or trust from becoming a party to any sale or pledge (for a loan, for example) of a beneficiary's interest, or to the claims of a beneficiary's creditors. Unless a specific provision to that effect is in a will or trust, an irresponsible beneficiary could waste his/her beneficial interest, even before it is received. Thus, the description of such a provision as a "spendthrift" clause.

Since it is easy enough to put the appropriate language in, it is foolish to leave it out. A typical spendthrift clause might state, "The interests of beneficiaries, until distributed, shall not be transferred, sold, pledged, or otherwise subject to the actions of such beneficiaries or to the claims of their creditors."

Bond Clauses

Probate and trust authorities in most if not all jurisdictions will require a "bond" of fiduciaries who administer an estate or trust. The bond is a form of insurance to protect the estate or trust and its beneficiaries against wrongdoing by the fiduciary; in that respect, the requirement is worthwhile.

But the cost of such a bond—usually renewable every year until the estate or trust administration is completed and the fiduciary discharged by the court—may be high. Your estate or trust will have to pay for the bond.

If you have named as fiduciary a person or institution in which your trust is complete and your confidence justifiable, you should add a provision to your will or trust stating that the fiduciary need not post a bond. Such a provision would say something like this: "I direct that no fiduciary acting hereunder shall be required to post a bond or other security in any jurisdiction in which he/she/it may act."

Such a provision will in most cases be honored, and the bond requirement waived. But if the fiduciary is outside the state in which your estate or trust is administered, or if significant assets in your estate or trust are in another state, the appropriate probate or trust authorities may nevertheless require a bond.

Again, if you have any fear that your fiduciary won't act properly, or that your beneficiaries will need the protection of a bond, you should reconsider naming that person as a fiduciary.

13

UPDATING YOUR WILL

As time passes, your desires, the tax laws, other people and your family situation change.

Which Will Counts?

It is important to keep in mind that a will is a transitory document. It can be changed at any time. Your latest will is the one that counts, no matter how many you have executed over the years. Your latest will may have been executed when your personal desires, the tax laws and your financial circumstances were very different. Your family and other people who have counted on you may be very surprised and disappointed—as you would be if you were still here.

When to Update

A will should not be a once-in-a-lifetime document. It should be reviewed periodically—at least every three years—to see whether what you wanted to accomplish when you executed it is still your desired plan.

For example, one of your children may have special problems for which you would now want to provide; one of your children may have married a spouse you don't trust or like; your own spouse may have experienced a medical problem which has impaired his/her judgment and capacity to make reasoned decisions; or you may have accumulated a great deal of wealth since you executed your last will. And there are many other changed circumstances which, when you take out your current will and read it, may cause you to realize that it is no longer appropriate.

After Moving to Another State

Another good reason to update your will is a move to another state. Since the requirements for form and content of wills and codicils, and the inheritance tax and property ownership laws in each state are unique, what you did when you lived in Pennsylvania may not be appropriate now that you have moved to California.

How to Update

Updating your will can be accomplished in two ways: You may have an entirely new will written, or you may have a codicil written.

Codicil

A codicil is an amendment which changes existing provisions of your will without re-doing the entire document. It is probably best, if you have more than one codicil, to have a new will drafted incorporating all of the changes. That is especially true in those states which have special requirements for codicils, the failure to comply with any of which may invalidate the changes you wanted to accomplish.

How to Revoke a Will

One way to revoke a will is simply to destroy it. This method is not necessarily the best. If you had an earlier will which still exists, it may become the effective one. Remember, it is your latest existing will which governs the disposition of your estate.

The best way to revoke a will is to write a new one. Most wills specifically state (and if they don't, they should) that all prior wills and codicils are revoked. That is the most intelligent way to proceed. However, once your new will is written and signed, it is a good idea to destroy all of your old wills, just to avoid confusion.

14

WHERE TO KEEP YOUR WILL

You should sign only *one* original copy of your will. A reason for this is that if you later decide to destroy your will, you may not be certain that you have destroyed all copies if there were more than one. Also, since you may only file one original for probate, there is absolutely no need to retain more than one, and only confusion could result if there was later uncertainty about your intentions.

Safe Deposit Box

The executed will should be kept where it is readily available to you, and/or to the person who will need to retrieve it when the time comes. It should also be in a place where it is completely safe from tampering or destruction. One such place may be a safe deposit box, but you should check the law of your state to see if there are any restrictions on access to a safe deposit box once a person has died. These restrictions may apply even if the box is in both your name and the name of another, still living, person.

With Your Lawyer

Another place to keep your will is in your lawyer's possession. Your lawyer ought to have either a fireproof safe in his/her office, or space for safekeeping in a bank vault.

No matter where the signed copy is kept, both you and your lawyer should keep a copy (unsigned) of your will available at all times.

A related bit of advice: You should keep with your will documents that show ownership of property, insurance, and other assets, and a list giving the location of important documents and items of property.

15

CHALLENGING A WILL

Legal Competence

When you make your will, you must be "legally competent." This means that your mental faculties must not be impaired and you must be able to understand your actions and their consequences. Also, you must not be subject to duress or the influence of another.

Disappointed heirs sometimes try to challenge a will on the grounds of legal incompetence. This means that even if no court procedings were ever initiated to have you declared incompetent, your will might be challenged on that ground.

"Under the Spell"

Similarly, if you executed your will when you were "under the spell" of a questionable person, or were in any way coerced to sign a will that did not reflect what you would have done had you been completely free to make your own choices, your will may be challenged and declared invalid.

Situations involving these issues sccm to arise most often when an elderly person falls under the influence of an individual who gains his or her confidence and then urges the person to have a new will prepared naming him or her as the beneficiary and/or executor. The influence or pressure may be subtle or blatant, and it may amount to "duress" if the elderly person becomes dependent on the individual for care, companionship, transportation or just "someone to talk to." A famous court battle over the estate of Groucho Marx involved just such a challenge. But the person need not be elderly, or disabled.

Proving incompetence, undue influence or duress may be difficult and costly. A court hearing, involving lawyers and medical and other "experts," may be necessary. It is difficult to win these cases because of the substantial burden of proof involved. Simply because a person of questionable capacity signs a new will which radically changes all previous estate planning, and which was prepared by a lawyer he or she has never met, does not mean automatically that the will is invalid.

If the will is declared invalid, then the next most recent will may be effective, and if there is no prior will, then the estate will be governed by the intestacy laws of the state.

16

WHAT HAPPENS IF YOU HAVE NO WILL, OR AN INVALID WILL?

There are two main results of dying without a will, or with a will that is determined to be invalid, for whatever reason, without another valid prior will.

No Choice and Higher Costs

The first consequence is that the manner in which your estate is distributed is determined under the laws of your state, rather than in accordance with your desires.

The second consequence is that the costs of administering your estate will very likely be higher, and the people responsible for administration will be appointed by a court or probate authority rather than individuals to whom you would have otherwise entrusted the responsibility.

Intestacy

If you leave no will, or if your will is held to be invalid, you will be considered to have died "intestate." There are intestacy laws in every state which dictate who will receive your property in that event. In most states, spouses and "lineal" descendants are preferred, which means that your husband or wife, parents, children, grandparents and grandchildren will be entitled to inherit from you in accordance with the priorities established by the laws of your state.

If you have no "heirs" in that category, then the intestate laws prescribe other relatives who will be entitled to inherit, such as sisters and brothers, aunts and uncles, nephews and nieces, and cousins.

No general statement can be made about the specific orders of priority, since the laws of each state vary. A general statement which can be made, however, is that it is always better to have a valid will than not to have one. Unless, of course, you don't care who gets what you have worked so hard to accumulate, and you don't care that less may remain for distribution because of higher administration costs.

A good example of the importance of a will involved a prominent lawyer who was unmarried and had no children. For years, he had promised his college, to which he was very devoted and generous, that it would receive his estate when he died. But he died without a will. The administration of his estate was very expensive; there was a battle over who would be the administrator; locating his assets was difficult; and his "family tree" had to be investigated. When it was all over, what was left passed to a distant relative in a faraway state whom he had not seen for several years. That was clearly not his wish, but that was the result required by the intestacy law.

PART III
PROBATE

17

WHAT IS PROBATE?

So much has been written about how you can handle your affairs to avoid the horror of probate, that we thought we would devote an entire section to setting the record straight.

"Reading of the Will"

You may have heard about, or seen in the movies, the "reading of the will," often portrayed as a moment of high drama. Family and other persons interested in the estate gather in an office to hear the lawyer slowly read the will.

That is sometimes still done, but it is not the norm and it is not required. Once a will is filed for probate, it becomes a matter of public record and anybody who wants to can read it for him/herself.

"Probate" is the legal process in which your estate is "administered" under the auspices and watchful eye of the court or other official legal entity charged with responsibility over such matters in your state. Remember that you will not be there to see that everything goes as you planned, so the courts have taken the responsibility to act on your behalf. Probate is the process by which this is accomplished.

What is "Administration"?

The administration of an estate is the process by which all of the deceased's accounts are settled, estate and/or inheritance taxes are paid, and assets are distributed to his/her beneficiaries/heirs.

45

Administration of an estate means several very important things. First, it means that your will is filed with the appropriate court or probate authority. Second, it means that once the will is filed, the executor(s) you name in your will is/are officially appointed by the court or probate authority and authorized to act as such in accordance with the terms of your will and applicable state laws.

Powers of the Executor

Once the executor is officially appointed, it is his/her duty to collect and identify all of your assets. The executor will also identify and pay your outstanding debts, funeral expenses and costs of administration (more on this later).

He/she will file the appropriate tax returns for you and for your estate. These include the "final life period" income tax returns (federal, state and local as may be appropriate), state inheritance tax returns (or returns, if there is also property of the decedent in another state which assesses tax on it), federal estate tax return (if your estate is large enough to require it), and ongoing income tax returns for the estate itself.

The executor will also have to file the required fiduciary reports or accountings which may be necessary under your state's laws, collect any money that was owed to you before your death, contest or settle claims against you or your estate and finally, distribute the remaining assets of your estate in accordance with the desires expressed in your will. If your estate is inadequate to satisfy all of your expressed desires, the executor will distribute the assets in accordance with the priorities established by the probate law of your state.

Appraisals

All assets which can't be immediately assigned a value (unlike cash, bank accounts and publicly traded securities) must be valued. In order to value them, they must sometimes be appraised by a qualified appraiser, and reported at fair market value for probate and tax reporting purposes.

What If There Is No Will?

Remember that if there is no will—that is, you die intestate (see Chapter 16)—then your estate is distributed in accordance with the intestacy law of your state, and the probate authority will appoint someone to administer your estate. That someone may be a relative, a bank or someone else appointed by the judge. You will never know who may get the job. The administrator who is appointed has all of the same responsibilities as an executor.

Costs of Administration

Administration costs seem to be the key item that everyone hopes to avoid when trying to circumvent probate.

It should not be surprising to you that your executor will receive a fee for services rendered. Administering an estate can be a time consuming and demanding job, and the person who does it with care and consideration should be compensated for his/her efforts.

It also should not be a cause of annoyance that other professionals who are hired by your executor (such as lawyers and accountants) receive a fee for services rendered to ensure that your estate is administered in accordance with the law and your wishes.

Other administration expenses may include court filing fees, legal advertising, appraisers' fees, brokers' fees, transfer charges (for stocks or real estate) and other costs of handling, owning, selling, or otherwise disposing of assets.

A Look at Dollars and Cents

Most state and some county probate courts or agencies have either official or unofficial schedules of allowable fees which are followed absent extraordinary circumstances. An example of an extraordinary circumstance is when an estate is sued in court by a disgruntled heir or someone with a claim and must spend money on its defense.

Following is an example of the unofficial guidelines for allowable fees in one jurisdiction:

Executor's Fees	*Attorney's Fees*
5% of first $100,000 of assets	7% of first $25,000 of assets
4% on next $100,000 of assets	6% of next $25,000 of assets
3% on next $100,000 of assets	5% of next $50,000 of assets
2% on assets in excess of $300,000	4% of next $100,000 of assets
	3% of assets in excess of $200,000

Hiring an Attorney

If you are an executor, you should first select as an attorney, if you choose to retain one, someone who has a good reputation and expertise in handling estates. You may want to interview more than one attorney. In the selection process, be sure to discuss fees. Once you select someone with whom you are comfortable, you should obtain an agreement detailing in writing your understanding of your arrangement.

Beware of a lawyer who "low-balls" his/her fee. As with most services which are "cheap," you usually get—or don't get—just what you pay for. And remember that if the lawyer charges on an hourly basis, someone with more expertise may charge more per hour, but have to spend fewer hours accomplishing the task.

Using the guidelines described above, if your estate were $100,000, the attorney would receive a fee of $5,750. Just to provide a comparison, your real estate broker would get more than that if he/she sold your house for $100,000 (a customary broker's fee is 6%), and he/she wouldn't have to prepare and file tax returns and reports for a court, collect assets, pay bills, settle claims and make distributions to heirs. If your executor negotiates a lower percentage fee, or agrees to pay the attorney an hourly fee, not to exceed the percentage limit, your beneficiaries could save money.

Executor's Fee

Your executor, especially if he/she is also a beneficiary, might also agree to take a lower fee, or no fee. That is something you might be able to arrange during your lifetime with a suitable document. But ask anyone who has ever served as an executor what he/she thought of the job and its responsibilities and you are likely to hear: "so much paperwork," "so many bills to pay," "so many trips to City Hall and the lawyer's office," "so many arguments in the family." It's no wonder that an executor receives compensation for this very difficult and time consuming job.

"After the Fees Are Paid—There's Nothing Left"

You have no doubt heard complaints that "after the executor and the lawyer got done with the estate, there was nothing left." That should never happen, but if it does, there are at least five possible causes:

1. The executor and/or the lawyer charged far more than was legal or appropriate. If so, the beneficiaries should complain to the court or probate authority. They might also file a complaint against the lawyer with the local bar association.
2. The deceased's affairs were in such disorder that it required extraordinary efforts to resolve claims, identify and obtain assets, mediate disputes among beneficiaries, settle taxes and fulfill legal responsibilities. You can avoid this problem if you follow the advice of your attorney, other professionals, and consider carefully the contents of this book.
3. The deceased owed a lot of taxes that should have been paid during his/her lifetime, or the taxes on the estate were so large (because of inadequate planning) that they ate up a good portion of the assets.
4. The decedent had so many debts that they consumed most or a large portion of the estate.
5. Somebody stole assets. In this case you should contact your local district attorney or county prosecutor immediately.

How Does All This Get Accomplished?

After the executor (or administrator if there is no will) finishes all the work that has to be done on the estate, he/she presents an accounting of what was done with the estate and a proposal for distribution. The court or probate authority examines the accounting, gives all interested parties an opportunity to challenge or question it at a hearing and, if everything is in order, approves the way the estate was handled and the way it is to be distributed.

The executor then distributes the assets to the beneficiaries according to the approved plan.

A Less Formal Method

The same result might be accomplished in a more informal, but no less legally binding, way in those jurisdictions where "family settlement agreements," or "estate settlement agreements," or whatever they are called where you live, are permitted. The executor still prepares an accounting. It lists all assets, what was done with them, what income was earned during the period of administration, what the deceased's debts were and how/when/whether they were paid, what the administration costs were, what's left and who gets it. It is incorporated in an agreement which approves the proposed distribution and releases the executor from all claims with respect to how the estate was administered.

Such an agreement is then signed by all parties who have a legal interest in the estate. When the assets are actually distributed, the beneficiaries will probably also be asked to sign receipts and releases which acknowledge that they received what they were entitled to, relieving the executor from future claims. If this can be done where you live, it could save your estate money and time.

18

AVOIDING PROBATE

Many people go to great lengths to avoid probate because they think they will "beat the system" and "save money." It often happens, though, that money is not saved, wishes are not fulfilled, and costs are nevertheless incurred, especially if there are assets which are forgotten in the process.

There are advantages and disadvantages to the various courses of action which may enable you to "avoid probate," and they ought to be very carefully considered before you take dramatic action which may not be un-doable. Remember that probate costs saved may be insignificant when compared to the costs to your independence, flexibility and ability to exert control over what you have taken a lifetime to accumulate.

Following are a few examples of ways to "avoid probate."

Living Trust

One way to avoid probate is by using a "living trust." You put all of your assets into a trust fund, administered by a trustee of your choice. The trustee pays you the income earned from investing your assets, gives you extra money or pays your bills as required, pays your funeral expenses and pays everything that's left when you die to the beneficiaries you name in the trust document.

The trustee may, and if it is a bank, will, charge fees every year for handling the trust. The trust has to file tax returns just as you do. More fees may be charged on its termination because it will be necessary to file an accounting with the court, and your estate—or the trust—may have to pay taxes on the assets when you die. And there are potential gift tax questions to consider.

So, theoretically, a living trust is a way to avoid probate, but have you really saved any money? Maybe not, when you add up the costs of setting up the trust (including the re-titling of property), the yearly costs of administration, and the final charges of the trustee. And, more important, you have lost control over your assets during the time such a trust is in existence. If it was an "irrevocable trust"—that is, one you can't cancel—you will have surrendered control for all time.

However, such a trust may be worthwhile and justified in certain circumstances. For example, 75-year old Sally Malone is widowed, has no children, and lives alone. She has a "living trust" prepared, naming the Midwest Bank to receive her assets, collect her income, pay her bills, give her money when she needs it and prepare her tax returns. When she dies the trustee will pay her last expenses and any taxes which may be due, file whatever must be filed under state law, and then distribute what's left to her nieces in San Diego.

The arrangement works well for Sally. The bank officer assigned cares about her and handles her affairs with sensitivity and competence. Of course, the bank charges an annual fee based on the principal and income, charges for preparation of tax returns, and will charge a fee for terminating the trust (and may hire a lawyer to represent it in the proceeding). Sally lives for 5 years under that arrangement. The costs may equal or exceed what "probate costs" would be, but she didn't do it to save probate costs. She did it for peace of mind, and she got it.

If you are thinking about such an arrangement, you should do it for the right reasons. And you should be aware of the disadvantages and costs, as well as the basic requirements of the bank you want to be trustee. A bank may require a certain level of assets before agreeing to serve. An individual could also be the trustee. You should be sure he/she knows what must be done and can do it. And you ought to be *very* sure that the individual is trustworthy, competent and sensible.

Joint Ownership

Another way to avoid probate is to transfer everything you own to the joint names of you and another person or persons, that is, create a "joint tenancy." This could result in a gift tax. But worse than that, the joint tenant could clean you out. How could that happen? Very easily. When you create a joint tenancy, both of the tenants legally own the entire asset. When one of you dies, the joint tenancy ends and the asset becomes the sole property of the survivor. But, since you both own the asset, it is possible for one joint tenant to cheat the other and to take the asset for his/her benefit. Your joint tenant could refuse to go along with your desires regarding how the asset is to be managed. If it is real estate or another asset which requires all joint owners to sign off in order to sell, the joint tenant could refuse.

In all probability there will be estate or inheritance taxes to be paid anyway, especially if the joint owner is not your spouse, on at least a half-interest in the joint property. That may not be true in all states, but it is a factor to consider.

Annuity

You could take everything you have and buy annuity policies. These are types of insurance policies which pay income to you for life and are payable at your death to your named beneficiaries. This might avoid probate, but gift and/or estate taxes might still be payable.

As to avoiding expenses: The insurance company from which you buy the annuity will certainly earn something from the transaction, so there are still costs involved in such an alternative. There is no such thing as free insurance.

Conclusion

Avoiding probate may be *a* goal, but it shouldn't be *the* goal in your planning process. In fact, the loss of flexibility and independence, plus the costs of trying to avoid it, may be more "expensive" than an orderly probate process. And the legal gymnastics you go through to "avoid probate" may raise more questions, and create more problems, than they resolve.

Actually, the only way to be certain that your assets will be handled, and your loved ones cared for, the way you want them to be is to execute a will, giving specific instructions to a trustworthy executor, and let the probate authority do what it was created to do—that is, see to it that your wishes are honored. Careful planning, such as negotiating fiduciary fees, can save as much money, if not more, than "avoiding probate."

PART IV
TAX PLANNING

19

FEDERAL ESTATE TAXES

Please note: The federal estate and gift tax laws were dramatically changed in 1981, and may change again. All of the information contained in this book is based on the laws existing at the time of writing, and is presented in the simplest way possible. The tax laws are very complicated, and tax planning should be accomplished by an expert.

Who Must Pay

As a practical matter, only a small percentage of people have to worry about federal estate taxes because the estate must be quite large to be taxable. Generally speaking, a Federal Estate Tax Return (Form 706) must be filed for the estates of people who die with "gross estates" exceeding $500,000 for 1986 and $600,000 for 1987 and thereafter.

These numbers are high, but don't automatically think that they do not apply to you. You may be surprised at the actual amount of your potential estate when you add up all the assets in which you have an interest, or over which you have control. The information solicited by the form in Appendix A will enable you to identify the assets which may constitute your "gross estate." Following are some of these assets:

- Real estate—residence or other
- Stocks
- Bonds
- Bank accounts—savings, checking, certificates of deposit

- Life insurance
- Pension or profit-sharing entitlements
- IRAs
- Keogh ("HR-10") funds
- Property held "in trust for" someone else
- Property held as "custodian for a minor"
- Property in another estate, or in a trust, to which you are entitled or the disposition of which you can control
- Business interests—whether corporate, partnership or proprietorship
- Investments in limited or other partnerships
- Personal property—such as jewelry, coin or stamp collections, antiques, automobiles, boats, household furnishings, artwork, and "collectibles"
- Salary or bonuses earned before death but not yet paid
- Annuities

Marital Deduction

The "marital deduction" means that property passing from one spouse to another is free from federal estate or gift tax.

Let's say that Horatio and Serena Applegate are married. If Horatio dies, and all his property passes to Serena, there will be no federal estate taxes to pay because of the marital deduction. However, when Serena dies, her estate, if it exceeds the minimums stated at the beginning of this chapter, may have to pay such taxes, unless there is some other reason why they can be avoided. That is the purpose of effective tax planning.

20

STATE INHERITANCE TAXES

Even if you are not subject to federal estate tax because your estate doesn't meet the federal minimum, your estate might still have to pay state inheritance or estate taxes.

If your estate includes property, particularly real estate, in a state other than the one in which you reside, inheritance taxes might have to be paid in that state, too. And there have been cases where the same property was taxed by two different states, each claiming that the deceased was a citizen of that state!

State inheritance tax laws are many and varied. For this reason, a competent professional should assist you in the planning process. The differences among the states can be radical. As an example, the tax rates may vary depending on the relationship of the beneficiary to the deceased. In one state the spouse and lineal descendants pay 6% tax, while all other beneficiaries pay 15%. And some states provide for deductions and exemptions in tax computation, while others do not.

21

GIFTS

Unified Credit/Exemption Equivalent

In 1981, Congress further revised, simplified, and integrated the estate and gift tax laws. It increased the "unified credit," thereby increasing the dollar amounts of estates and gifts which could pass free of tax. The unified credit is a lifetime advantage. All or parts of the credit can be used by your estate and/or for gifts during your lifetime.

A key figure related to the unified credit is the "exemption equivalent"—the aggregate total of your estate and lifetime gifts which, thanks to the unified credit, can pass free of tax. The exemption equivalent is $500,000 in 1986 and $600,000 in 1987 and thereafter. This figure applies to the dollar value of your net estate *plus* the total of all taxable gifts that you made during your lifetime. (Taxable gifts refer to any gift not subject to an exclusion or exemption.)

For example, someone who dies in 1987, with lifetime taxable gifts and a net estate totaling $600,000, would pay no federal estate tax. At that amount, the unified credit exactly offsets the tax due.

If, however, your net estate and taxable gifts exceed the exemption equivalent, you first compute tax on the total amount of your net estate and taxable gifts and then apply the unified credit against the tax so computed. The unified credit is $155,800 for 1986 and $192,800 for 1987 and thereafter. A Unified Gift and Estate Tax Rate Schedule is provided in Appendix B.

Gifts

An individual can make gifts worth $10,000 *each year* (annual exclusion) to any number of individuals. So, ten gifts of $10,000 each to ten different people—or a total of $100,000—will not result in gift tax. And, if your spouse joins in these gifts, their amount can be doubled—to $20,000 per recipient, per year. Amounts in excess of these limits are "taxable gifts."

Lifetime gifts can be utilized as an important estate planning tool, whether or not your estate is subject to federal estate tax, by helping avoid state inheritance taxes. However, some states tax gifts made within a certain period before death (commonly 1, 2, 3 years or more). If you can avoid these time frames, you might just avoid all taxes.

Interest-Free Loans

It used to be possible to lend money or other assets without interest. The borrower received the income from the asset and could have sold it at a profit (if it appreciated in value). His/her only responsibility was to return the original dollar value of the loan. This resulted in tax on the income or profits at the borrower's lower rate and, at the end of the loan period, the original value of the asset(s) was returned to the "lender" without tax consequence.

The Tax Reform Act of 1984 effectively eliminated this device. Both interest-free and below-market interest loans are now considered to be loans made at an *assumed* rate of interest (determined by the IRS). The lender is taxed on the interest so imputed and is considered to have made a gift of the interest to the borrower.

There are very limited exceptions: One is that the adverse income and gift tax consequences do not apply if the total of *all* outstanding loans (those with interest and those without) between the individuals is not greater than $10,000. You should consult your tax advisor before making any "interest-free" loans.

22

CHILDREN

Uniform Gifts To Minors Act ("UGMA")

Every state (and D.C.) has a law which provides that gifts can be made to minors (children under 18 or the age fixed by the state's law, up to 21) which result in shifting income to the minor and transferring ownership of the property to the minor when he/she reaches the age of majority.

Such transfers are subject to federal gift tax rules: individual gifts in excess of $10,000 in any year are taxable gifts.

Custodian

Transfers under the UGMA require a "custodian" for the minor. In most states the custodian can be any adult you choose, but (1) if the income from your gift is used to satisfy your obligation of support for the child (which may include the cost of college education in some states), you will be taxed on the income; and (2) if you, the giver of the gift, are also the custodian, the value of the fund will be subject to federal estate tax, and possibly state inheritance tax, in your estate.

So if you are contemplating gifts to minors under the UGMA to reduce your taxable estate, you should not be the custodian. A custodian, like a guardian, should be carefully selected. Also, it is a good idea to appoint a successor custodian.

Irrevocability

A gift made under the UGMA is irrevocable. Once you transfer the property to the custodian who holds the property for the child, you can't get it back. As soon as the child reaches the age of majority, he/she will own the property outright.

Many people prefer that their children not own significant assets upon reaching majority. There may be concern that funds which were intended to be used for extra education, or buying a business, or buying a home, will instead be spent on fast cars and/or questionable activities. If that is a realistic fear, you should reconsider whether you wish to make UGMA gifts.

Transferring Property

People often use the UGMA to transfer property expected to appreciate in value. If the property is later sold at a profit, the tax will be payable by the minor at a rate determined by the age of the minor (see below).

The Importance of Age 14

The income from the UGMA gift, whether paid out or left to accumulate, will be reportable by the minor on his/her tax return. Under the Tax Reform Act of 1986, the rate at which unearned income is taxed depends on the age of the minor. Minors age 14 and over are taxed on unearned income at their own tax rate, but those under age 14 are taxed in large part at their parents' top tax rate.

Unearned Income Under Age 14

"Unearned income" includes income from savings accounts, trusts, custodial accounts under the Uniform Gifts to Minors Act, etc., etc. "Net unearned income" is defined as unearned income *less* a) up to $500 of the child's "standard deduction," or b) the full amount of itemized deductions in excess of the "2% floor" specifically attributable to unearned income. In general, all net unearned income of a child under age 14 in excess of the first $500, from whatever source, is taxed as if it had been added to the parents' income, if the parents' tax rate is higher than the child's.

Since the child may take a standard deduction of up to $500 against unearned income, the tax on the unearned income of a child under 14 works as follows:

UNEARNED INCOME	TAX RATE
0–$500	None (standard or itemized deduction)
$500–1,000	Child's rates
Over 1,000	Higher of parents' or child's rates

It is important to note that gifts prior to 1987 are *not* excluded from the foregoing rules, and that a child eligible to be claimed as a dependent on his/her parent's return is not permitted to claim the personal exemption on his/her own return.

Financing Education

Traditional income-shifting techniques, a major way to build up money to finance education, have been swept away by the 1986 Act, which specifically disallows Clifford and spousal remainder trusts and eliminates the tax advantage of other methods. (See Chapter 23.) However, remember that the unearned income of a child age 14 or older is not taxed at the parents' rate. Parents may want to think of investing for children in assets such as Series EE U.S. Savings Bonds, on which earnings are not taxable until maturity or redemption, with the investment planned so that the maturity dates arrive after the child attains age 14.

Remember that for many individuals the drop in tax rates under the new law will reduce the tax bite on all investment income, other than capital gains, so that income can be earned and accumulated for the future with less need to look for specific tax breaks.

23

TRUSTS

A trust is a kind of fictional legal "person." It is an entity which, when established, is capable of owning and distributing assets and income. There are two basic categories of trusts: those created during one's lifetime (called "inter vivos"), and those created in one's will (called "testamentary").

Ways Trusts Are Used

Trusts are used for many reasons, and not only for estate planning. They are often used to provide for people who may need help during their lifetime: for example, a child or elderly relative. Trusts may take the place of outright gifts to people who cannot handle their money or property responsibly. And trusts sometimes can be used to save taxes.

Trustee

All trusts are managed by one or more trustees. It is the trustee who is actually responsible for the day-to-day management of the trust assets and who carries out the wishes of the person who established the trust.

Who Should Be a Trustee

A trustee must be a person, or a bank or other entity legally permitted to so act, capable of managing assets, keeping good records, and filing necessary tax returns and court reports. (See Chapter 11.)

You can name more than one trustee, and you can have language in your will or trust document stating how and when a trustee can be replaced.

For example, let's say that you name as trustee your friend, Sharon, because she is trustworthy and sensitive to the needs of the trust beneficiaries. But Sharon just isn't too good with numbers. You can in this case name both Sharon and the Rainbow Valley Bank as co-trustees, and give Sharon the power to replace Rainbow Valley with another bank, if they disagree on the management of the trust, or if the bank's investments are bad or, if you like, for absolutely no cause at all.

You must remember that managing a trust takes a lot of time, responsibility and paperwork. You might want to include a professional (such as a bank) as a co-trustee to ease the burden on your other trustee(s) and to provide expert guidance.

Advantages and Disadvantages of Trusts

A common complaint about a trust, and perhaps one that in some circumstances is both a disadvantage and an advantage, is that the beneficiary of the trust has no control over its assets. Spouses for whom funds are left in trust often complain that they have to ask for money rather than having it as their own. This may be correct, if that is what the trust document says. Depending on the situation, and the intentions/expectations of the person who established the trust, that could be good or bad.

Another disadvantage is that trusts can be costly to create and maintain.

Use of Trusts in Estate Tax Planning

But trusts can be extremely useful in estate tax planning, if your assets are large enough to make them worthwhile. Here is an example:

Marvin and Helene Jones (who made no taxable gifts during their lives) have the following assets which would, if they died soon, constitute their estate:

ASSETS	HOW OWNED		
	Marvin	Helene	Joint
Residence			$150,000
Stocks and bonds	$100,000	$ 50,000	100,000
Money market accounts	100,000	50,000	50,000
Profit-sharing account	200,000		
Certificates of deposit	100,000		
TOTALS	$500,000	$100,000	$300,000

If Marvin died on January 1, 1987, and his will left everything to Helene, his gross estate would be $650,000 ($500,000 individually-owned assets and half of $300,000 jointly-owned assets).* No federal estate tax would be due because of the "marital deduction" (see Chapter 19).

But if Helene then died on June 1, 1987, had not remarried, and had not used up any of her own assets or the assets she received from Marvin, her estate would have to pay substantial federal estate tax:

Helene's taxable estate	=	$ 900,000
Tentative tax on $900,000	=	306,800
Less: unified credit	=	192,800
TAX DUE	=	$ 114,000

This means that Marvin and Helene's children or other beneficiaries would receive net assets of $786,000 ($900,000 estate less $114,000 tax due). But if Marvin's will had set up a trust for Helene, into which the maximum "exemption equivalent" (see Chapter 21) was put, and the trust assets were payable to the named beneficiaries at Helene's death, there would have been no federal estate tax payable in *either* estate. The beneficiaries would have received $114,000 more. Such a trust must be very carefully prepared if this is to work. If your assets are large enough to make it worthwhile, you should consider it—and discuss it with your spouse and your lawyer.

*We have assumed that there were no administration expenses or state inheritance taxes, just to illustrate the point.

Lifetime Trusts

Lifetime trusts ("inter vivos") may be used to save estate taxes only if you effectively part with all ownership and control of, and all beneficial interest in, the property you transfer to such trusts.

Keep in mind that the establishment of trusts for the benefit of others during your lifetime may create taxable gifts if you exceed the $10,000 per person annual exclusion.

Clifford Trusts and Spousal Remainder Trusts

Clifford and spousal remainder trusts, which used to provide methods for shifting taxable income to children and other dependents or relatives taxed at lower tax rates, can no longer be established under the Tax Reform Act of 1986. Any such trusts established before March 1, 1986 retain their tax benefits. But new Clifford or spousal remainder trusts are effectively ruled out after that date.

Under the previous law, a Clifford trust had to last for more than 10 years and provide that the trust assets (called the "corpus") return to the trust creator (the "grantor") when the trust ended in order to shift taxable income to the beneficiary. But the 1986 law states that if the grantor retains an ultimate interest in the trust assets (called a "reversionary" interest) of more than 5% of the value of the trust, the income from the trust will be taxed at the grantor's tax rate. This has effectively eliminated Clifford trusts as income-shifting devices.

A spousal remainder trust can last for *any* term of years. The grantor establishes a trust giving trust income to a named beneficiary, usually his/her child, and providing that the trust assets will pass to the grantor's spouse at the end of the term. The 1986 law states that if the grantor and his/her spouse were living together at the time the trust was created, and if the trust assets were transferred to the trust after March 1, 1986, the trust income will be taxed at the grantor's rate. This makes a spousal remainder trust ineffective as an income-shifting technique.

However, spousal remainder trusts, unlike Clifford trusts, may still have positive estate tax consequences: the property placed in trust is removed from the grantor's estate, since there is no way he/she can get the property back.

Existing Clifford and Spousal Remainder Trusts

The law allows Clifford and spousal remainder trusts established and funded before March 1, 1986, to retain their income-shifting benefits. Keep in mind, however, that unearned income of a child under age 14 is subject to the less favorable new tax rules no matter when such a trust was created. See Chapter 22.

Charitable Trusts

Property may be kept out of your estate for tax purposes if you establish trusts where charities are the ultimate beneficiaries of the trust property. The rules are very complicated, and great care must be taken to draft documents which meet the very strict tests of eligibility. Such trusts may also be created by your will.

Here are some of the types of trusts you may want to consider:

Charitable Remainder Trust

A charitable remainder trust provides that income is paid to a beneficiary (or beneficiaries) which are not qualified "charities" for the life of that beneficiary or for a fixed term of years. Then either the trust continues to exist for the benefit of a qualified charity, or the assets of the trust (called the "remainder interest") are paid to the charity outright.

The trust itself (but not the beneficiary) is exempt from income taxation, and the person who establishes the trust may be entitled to a charitable deduction for income tax, gift tax or estate tax purposes. The trust may not be revoked. Once it is established, the person who created it cannot end it or get his/her property back. There are at least two kinds of charitable remainder trusts:

(1) A charitable remainder unitrust, which annually pays a predetermined percentage (not less than 5%) of the net value of its assets, as valued each year, to a beneficiary(s) who is not a charity.

(2) A charitable remainder annuity trust, which annually pays a fixed sum to a beneficiary(s) who is not a charity. However, the fixed sum must not be less than 5% of the value of the property on the date it was transferred to the trust.

Charitable Income Trust

A charitable income trust provides that trust income is paid to a qualified charity for some predetermined period of time (measured either in years or by some standard such as "for the life of Brian"), after which the principal (corpus) of the trust either comes back to the grantor, or is paid to another noncharity beneficiary. There are a great many complicated rules which must be satisfied if the potential charitable deduction benefits are to be gained.

Many public charities have set up their own charitable trusts, and it may be easier to use them. If you are in a position to consider such charitable trusts, you should obtain independent financial or tax advice on their benefits and risks. You should most especially be sure that the "charity" is indeed a qualified entity eligible for the potentially favorable tax treatment.

24

TRUST TAXATION

The Tax Reform Act of 1986 changed the taxation of trusts in many significant ways.

Taxation of Grantor Trusts

A "grantor" trust is a trust established by a donor who retains benefits from or control over it. Such benefits can include the right to receive income, or the right to receive the trust property upon expiration of a certain term or upon the happening of certain events (if such right to get the property back is more than a 5% possibility). A trust which contains the right of the donor to revoke it and get the trust property back is also a "grantor" trust.

The consequence of being a grantor trust, as determined under the provisions of the Internal Revenue Code, is that all income, whether distributed to beneficiaries (who may or may not include the grantor) or accumulated by the trust, is taxable to the grantor at his/her tax rates. A further consequence is that income or principal distributed to beneficiaries will constitute a gift from the grantor.

Taxation of Nongrantor Trusts

The new tax law imposes new tax rates on nongrantor trusts, with respect to undistributed income, starting in 1987. Here are the new tax rate schedules:

1987:

Taxable Income		Tax
More than	But not more than	
$ 0	$ 500	11%
500	4,700	$55 plus 15% of excess over $500
4,700	7,550	$685 plus 28% of excess over $4,700
7,550	15,150	$1,483 plus 35% of excess over $7,550
more than	$15,150	$4,143 plus 38.5% of excess over $15,150

1988 and thereafter:

Taxable Income		Tax
More than	But not more than	
$ 0	$ 5,000	15%
5,000	13,000	$750 plus 28% of excess over $5,000
13,000	26,000	$2,990 plus 33% of excess over $13,000
more than	$26,000	28%

Taxable Year

The new law specifically states that all trusts, whether currently in existence or as yet to be created, must use the calendar year for tax reporting. Charitable trusts are exempt from this requirement.

Quarterly Estimated Tax Payments

Beginning in 1987, all trusts must make quarterly estimated tax payments, just like individuals. Estates are subject to the same rule, but are exempt from the requirement for their first two years.

Clifford and Spousal Remainder Trusts

The law allows Clifford and spousal remainder trusts created before March 1, 1986, to retain their income-

72

shifting benefits, so that distributed income will continue to be taxed at the beneficiary's rate. See Chapter 23.

Generation-Skipping Tax

The new law tightens the application of the generation-skipping tax—an additional tax paid when individuals receive gifts or bequests from persons who are more than one generation older than the recipient. In practice, this tax applies only to extremely wealthy people and to very large gifts or bequests.

Through 1989, a person may give up to $2,000,000 to each grandchild (in trust or outright) without incurring the generation-skipping tax, so long as there is no intervening beneficiary. In addition, there is a $1,000,000 exemption for any generation-skipping transfers where there is an intervening beneficiary (such as: to son for life, then to grandson). After 1989, the $2,000,000-per-grandchild exclusion is eliminated.

PART V
LIFETIME TAX
PLANNING

25

GET ORGANIZED

A will is, of course, the most obvious form of "lifetime" estate planning. It is, however, only one part of the process.

You must also plan and organize your affairs so that there will be an orderly, tax-effective disposition of assets after you die. How property is owned, for example, may determine who receives it. You may have money in a joint bank account with your son. It will pass automatically to him at your death, no matter what your will says. If you own real estate "in trust for" your daughter, it will probably pass to her upon your death whether or not that was your intention. And unless your will is properly drafted, others may bear the tax burdens for assets they do not receive.

Chapters 25–27 describe some areas of estate planning which, in addition to will drafting, should be attended to during your lifetime.

Retirement Plans

You must think about how your interests in retirement plans, including pension, profit-sharing, "Keogh", 401(k) plans and IRAs, will be treated at your death. If you signed a beneficiary designation when you enrolled in the plan, make sure that it still reflects your wishes. The beneficiary designation, and not your will, will determine who is to receive your interests in such plans, unless your estate is the beneficiary. And even if your plan benefits do not pass through your estate and under your will, they may nevertheless be subject to estate and/or inheritance tax.

For more information on retirement plans, see the No-Nonsense Financial Guide, *How to Plan and Invest for Your Retirement.*

Life Insurance

It is remarkable how forgetful people can be when it comes to life insurance. We know of one situation where a person's former husband was still the beneficiary of her life insurance more than eight years after their divorce!

You should review every life insurance policy you have, including those provided by your employer, trade association, professional or other group. Include your estate planning lawyer in the process. If you have the "incidents of ownership," which means that you can control the beneficiary designation, have borrowing power, and the right to receive cash value, the policy will become part of your taxable estate, at least for federal purposes.

If your beneficiary designations are no longer appropriate—change them. But before changing them, ask your lawyer for suggestions. He/she may, for example, recommend that you can avoid paying estate taxes if you transfer ownership of an insurance policy to another person—perhaps the insurance beneficiary. You might then give that person a gift each year equal to the policy premium for the beneficiary to pay. Or, your lawyer may recommend establishing a trust as the beneficiary of the policy proceeds.

What is most important is consideration and thorough planning.

26

BUSINESS INTERESTS

What will happen to your business when you die? Is there a buy-sell agreement which allows your partner(s) to buy your share from your estate or beneficiary? If not, will your estate be able to sell your interest? If you have significant responsibility in managing the business, is there someone to replace you?

Every business situation is unique, but here are a few suggestions.

Proprietorship

If you own your business as a proprietorship (that is, not in partnership nor in corporate form) you should have someone—your spouse, accountant, or lawyer—who knows how it runs. They should know your principal customers, suppliers and creditors, and where all the important records are kept. You should tell them about likely candidates to purchase the business, if it is to be sold after your death. If you expect the business to continue, you should have someone ready to step in and run it.

Careful thought should be given to how you treat your business in your will. Whoever is the business beneficiary will have the responsibilities of ownership. The person should be capable of accepting or responsibly delegating them. For this reason, you should give serious thought to who should receive it and on what terms.

Partnership

If you own a business in partnership with another person or persons, your signed partnership agreement should cover the disposition of each partner's interest at death. This provision should be drafted to meet the needs of both the partnership business as well as the individual partners. It should contain price and payment terms that are acceptable to everyone, if a buy-out is required.

You should examine your partnership agreement to be sure that the needs of you and your partners are met in the event of the death of any one of you.

If you do not have a partnership agreement, have one prepared. There are at least two reasons to have an agreement: Some states require a partnership to be dissolved upon the death of one partner unless otherwise provided, and, absent agreed terms, the buy-out of a deceased partner's interest is almost guaranteed to generate problems and expense for everyone.

Corporation

If your business is owned in corporate form, where you are the sole shareholder, the issues are similar to those for a proprietorship. But if there are other shareholders, your problems will be more similar to those of a partnership.

The best way to dispose of corporate shares upon the death of a shareholder is to prepare a shareholders' agreement. The agreement should set a fixed dollar amount or agreed-upon formula for determining price, and include payment terms. The agreement should be reviewed periodically to make sure that the price and payment terms are still agreeable to everyone.

Review Regularly

It is a good idea to review partnership and shareholder agreements regularly because relationships, capacities, and businesses can change. The agreements, which should not only deal with buy-outs at death, but also retirement, disability, termination and responsibilities, should always be reviewed in the estate planning process.

80

27

POWERS OF ATTORNEY AND "LIVING WILLS"

Powers of Attorney

Powers of attorney, which may be "general" or "limited," are documents by which you authorize another person (or persons, or entity) to act on your behalf.

General Power of Attorney

A general power of attorney gives the person or entity you designate (called your "attorney-in-fact") authority to do whatever you can do. This includes the power to sign checks, make deposits, hire attorneys and accountants, pay bills, pursue and settle claims, buy and sell property, sign and file tax returns, and almost anything else you can do for yourself. Such powers are given in a variety of circumstances—for example, if you are having an operation, or taking an extended trip, and you want someone to manage your affairs. Some people use them who just don't want to be bothered with managing their finances.

Since a general power of attorney is so broad, you should carefully consider whether you want to delegate so much authority, and whether the attorney-in-fact is completely honest, trustworthy and able. Such a power can only be granted while you are competent—that is, you have control of your senses, awareness of what you are doing, and freedom from undue influence or duress when you grant it.

Unless you specifically state otherwise in the document itself, in many if not most states, a power of attorney—general or limited—will not be effective after you *become* incompetent. To avoid that result, you should have a "durable" power of attorney, which says that your subsequent incompetence does not invalidate the powers granted.

Limited Power of Attorney

A limited power of attorney grants authority to the attorney-in-fact only to take specific actions, and/or for a limited period of time. For example: You are buying a vacation home in Wyoming, but you don't want to travel to Laramie for the closing. A limited power of attorney could be used to authorize the person you name to attend the closing and sign the necessary ownership documents (the mortgage, note, affidavits, closing cost sheet, etc.). Or, you will be away on vacation for four weeks and you expect some checks and bills to come in. You can authorize your attorney-in-fact to make deposits and sign the checks to pay your bills during that time.

Most banks, brokerage houses, government agencies and others who will be asked to rely on your power of attorney will require originals or copies of the document. They should be contacted first to ascertain what their requirements are.

"Living Wills"

A "living will" is something of a misnomer. It is not a will in the usual sense—it doesn't dispose of property, establish trusts, talk about taxes or authorize a fiduciary to represent your estate.

A living will is more like a power of attorney: It authorizes a person or persons to make critical decisions for you in special circumstances where you are either so ill or so injured that decisions must be made about using "heroic measures" to keep you alive.

A living will grants specific authority to someone to make the decision to terminate artificial prolongation of life, and states that doctors, hospitals and others relying on such a decision may do so without fear of legal reprisal.

Not all states have legally authorized living wills as a basis for terminating life support in otherwise hopeless cases. If the issue is of concern to you, your attorney can tell you whether your state sanctions such documents or whether they have been accepted in practice.

28

CONCLUSION

Estate Planning should not be a mystery. With good professional help and serious thought, the complexities can be competently handled. What is most important is that your wishes be fulfilled in a way which eases the burden on your family and minimizes possible arguments.

Planning your estate is something you should approach the way you might plan your vacation—where is your estate to go, and how will it get there. This book provides a road map. You have to make the decisions.

Estate planning really doesn't take very much time, and its cost is small compared to its value. When you think about how hard you've worked to acquire what you have, and when you think about wanting to provide for your loved ones—it makes a whole lot of sense to go about it the right way.

GLOSSARY

Accounting The report prepared by a fiduciary of an estate or trust, detailing assets and income received, expenses paid, and distributions made or proposed to be made.

Administrator The fiduciary appointed by the court or probate authority to handle the administration of an estate when there is no will, or an invalid will.

Antenuptial Agreement An agreement entered into by two people before they marry detailing rights and/or obligations in case of divorce or death.

Beneficiary A person or entity named in a will or trust to receive income and/or assets.

Bequest A disposition or gift given in a will.

Bond (Fiduciary Bond) A type of insurance policy purchased by a trust or estate to protect against loss or wrongdoing by a fiduciary.

Codicil An amendment to a will.

Contingent Beneficiary A person or entity who becomes a beneficiary of a will or trust because of the occurence of a specified event or upon the death or disqualification of a named beneficiary.

Corpus (or "Principal") The assets of a trust.

Estate The total assets owned by a person at the time of death.

Estate Tax Federal or State tax payable on the value of an estate.

Executor/Executrix The person or entity named in a will to administer an estate.

Fiduciary An executor, administrator, trustee, guardian, custodian, or any other person or entity entrusted with assets held for the benefit of others.

Gift Tax Tax payable on non-exempt gifts (exemptions can occur because of the $10,000 annual exclusion and the "unified credit").

Grantor A person who establishes and contributes assets to a trust.

Guardian A person or entity named in a will or appointed by a court to be responsible for the property and/or person of minors or incompetents.

Heir A person who receives assets from an estate. Specifically, a person who, under state law, inherits all or part of an estate of someone who dies intestate.

Holographic Will   A handwritten will.

Inheritance Tax   Tax payable to a state on the value of an estate or on specific property of a decedent.

Intangible Property   Property which has no value of its own, but is the representation of value, such as shares of stock or bond certificates.

Inter Vivos   A Latin term meaning "between the living," that is, something done by a living person, as opposed to an act done by a will.

Intestacy/Intestate   The state of dying without a will, or without a valid will.

Irrevocable   An act which cannot be revoked, recalled or cancelled. The money or property placed in an irrevocable trust, for example, cannot be taken back by the grantor.

Issue   Lineal descendants, that is, children, grandchildren, great-grandchildren, etc.

Lapse   The cancellation of a bequest because of the death of the named beneficiary or the happening of another specified event.

Legal Competence   The capacity to act on one's own behalf without mental or other disability.

Life Estate   A person's interest in property or other asset, the duration of which is limited to his/her lifetime.

Liquid Asset   An asset which is readily convertible into cash.

Living Trust   A trust established during a person's lifetime.

Personal Property   Property other than real property; can be tangible or intangible.

Prenuptial Agreement   See Antenuptial Agreement.

Probate   The process of filing and proving the validity of a will and administering the will under the supervision of a court or probate authority.

Real Estate   See Real Property.

Real Property   Land and buildings.

Residual Estate   See Residue.

Residue   What is left of an estate after all debts, expenses and specific bequests are paid.

Self-proving Will   A will which conforms to certain rules pertaining to its execution that can be probated without having witnesses appear to confirm their signatures.

Spendthrift   A person who does not wisely manage assets and spends them foolishly.

Spendthrift Trust   A trust established to protect assets of or for someone considered a spendthrift.

Tangible Property   Property which you can hold or touch, such as automobiles, furniture, and jewelry.

Taxable Estate   The value of an estate on which taxes are paid; determined after claiming all allowable deductions, exclusions, and exemptions.

Testator/Testatrix   A person who makes and executes a will.

Trust   A legal entity created to hold and deal with property for the benefit of specified persons or entities.

Trustee   A person or entity responsible for carrying out the terms of a trust.

Unified Credit   An amount ($155,800 in 1986, and $192,800 in 1987 and thereafter) of credit which may be taken against total gift and estate taxes owed.

Unified Credit Exemption Equivalent   The dollar amount of the gifts and the estate which is not taxed because of the Unified Credit ($500,000 in 1986, and $600,000 in 1987 and thereafter).

Will   The legal document by which a person disposes of his/her estate.

APPENDIX A:
NO-NONSENSE ESTATE PLANNING INFORMATION SUMMARY

PERSONAL DATA

FAMILY

Name	Social Security Number	Date of Birth	Relationship	Address and Phone	Comments

FINANCIAL DATA

BANKING INFORMATION

Company Name	Address	Contact Person	Account	
			Type	Number

Safe Deposit Box

Co-Signatory	Location	Number

INSURANCE INFORMATION

Company Name	Address	Contact Person

Tables for listing exact assets and liabilities follow. Enter here information needed in contacting appropriate parties in respect to your personal business dealings.

INVESTMENT INFORMATION

Broker/Advisor Name	Address	Account	
		Type	Number

OTHER ADVISORS, ACCOUNTANTS, ATTORNEYS

Name	Address	Telephone

ASSETS

Type	Description	Form of Ownership*	Value	Documents Located at
REAL ESTATE				
PERSONAL PROPERTY				

*Who owns and how (solely, jointly with ———, in trust for ———, custodian for ———, etc.)

Type/Name	Description	Form of Ownership	Value	Documents Located At
BANK ACCOUNTS AND OTHER INVESTMENTS				
NOTES RECEIVABLE, EXPECTANCIES, COPYRIGHTS, LICENSES, PATENTS, AND ANY OTHER INTANGIBLE ASSETS				

DEFERRED COMPENSATION

Type	Name of Plan/Employer	Account Balance	Form of Benefit	Beneficiary
Unfunded Plans				
Pension Plans				
Profit-Sharing Plans				
Keogh Plans				
IRAs				
Employee Savings Plans				
Deferred Bonus or Salary				

LIFE INSURANCE

Company	Policy #	Face Amount	Insured	Owner	Beneficiary

TRUSTS*

Grantor	Beneficiary	Interest of Beneficiary	Principal Value	Annual Income	Distribution Date

*If you have the right to designate who will be entitled to receive assets or income from an estate or trust, identify them by name, describe the nature of the power, and estimate the value of the assets which are subject to your power.

OTHER ASSETS (Describe Nature, Value, Form of Ownership and Location)

LIABILITIES

Company or Person to Whom Owed	Payee or Account or Policy #	Amount Due	When Payable
Mortgages			
Auto, Boat, or other secured loan			
Unsecured Loans and credit lines			
Insurance Loans			
Other Indebtedness			
Guarantees and other Contingent Liabilities			
Child Support			
Alimony			
OTHER LIABILITIES (college, health care, parental support, and so forth, whether anticipated or current)			

MISCELLANY

CURRENT WILL
Date
Location

FIDUCIARIES	Name	Address	Phone	Relationship	Note
Executor(s)					
Successor Executor(s)					
Trustee(s)					
Successor Trustee(s)					
Guardian(s)					
Successor Guardian(s)					

Use "Note" column if making change for new will or for any other relevant information.

LIFETIME GIFTS PREVIOUSLY REPORTED (Attach copies of Gift Tax Returns)

APPENDIX B

TAXABLE GIFTS OR ESTATE

Here is the unified gift and estate tax rate schedule in effect for 1987:

(1) On amounts more than	(2) But not more than	(3) Tax on amount in column (1)	(4) Tax rate on amounts exceeding column (1)
$ -0-	$ 10,000	$ -0-	18%
10,000	20,000	1,800	20%
20,000	40,000	3,800	22%
40,000	60,000	8,200	24%
60,000	80,000	13,000	26%
80,000	100,000	18,200	28%
100,000	150,000	23,800	30%
150,000	250,000	38,800	32%
250,000	500,000	70,800	34%
500,000	750,000	155,800	37%
750,000	1,000,000	248,300	39%
1,000,000	1,250,000	345,800	41%
1,250,000	1,500,000	448,300	43%
1,500,000	2,000,000	555,800	45%
2,000,000	2,500,000	780,800	49%
2,500,000	3,000,000	1,025,800	53%
3,000,000		1,290,800	55%

Starting in 1988, the rate schedule is as follows (using the same column headings):

$ -0-	$ 10,000	$ -0-	18%
10,000	20,000	1,800	20%
20,000	40,000	3,800	22%
40,000	60,000	8,200	24%
60,000	80,000	13,000	26%
80,000	100,000	18,200	28%
100,000	150,000	23,800	30%
150,000	250,000	38,800	32%

250,000	500,000	70,800	34%
500,000	750,000	155,800	37%
750,000	1,000,000	248,300	39%
1,000,000	1,250,000	345,800	41%
1,250,000	1,500,000	448,300	43%
1,500,000	2,000,000	555,800	45%
2,000,000	2,500,000	780,800	49%
2,500,000		1,025,800	50%

	UNIFIED CREDIT	EXEMPTION EQUIVALENT
1985	$121,800	$400,000
1986	155,800	500,000
1987 and thereafter	192,800	600,000

INDEX

final accounting of estate, 50
powers of, 46
see also Fiduciary(ies)
Executrix, defined, 85
Exemption equivalent, 67
Expenses, payment of, 32, 46

Family, role in disposition of assets, 10
Federal estate tax minimum, exceeding, 22
Federal Estate Tax Return Form 706, 57
Fee(s), 29
administration, 47-48
unofficial guidelines, 48
Fiduciary(ies), 16
choice of, 29
defined, 9, 26, 85
fees, 29
powers of, 27
qualities of, 26
specific and broad powers of, 28
standard of care, 28
successor, 26
Fiduciary bonds, 33-34
"Final life period" income tax returns, 27, 46
401(k) plan, 77

Generation-skipping tax, 73
Gift(s)
irrevocable, 62-63
lifetime, 61
prior to 1987, 64
taxable, 60, 97
Gift tax, 53
defined, 85
marital deduction, 58
Grantor(s), 68
defined, 85
Grantor trusts, 71
"Gross estate," 57
Guardian(s), 30
appointment of, 17
consent of designated, 30
defined, 85
successor, 30-31
see also Fiduciary(ies)

Heir(s)
challenging will, 39
defined, 8, 85
see also Beneficiary(ies)
Holographic will, 14
ambiguity of, 14
defined, 86
problems of, 14

Illegitimate children, as beneficiary, 23-24

Income-shifting technique(s), 64
spousal remainder trust as, 68
Incompetence, proving, 40
Inexpensive will, 4-5
Inheritance tax, 19, 32
defined, 86
joint ownership, 53
state, 59
tangible personal property, 19
Intangible property, 17
defined, 86
Interest-free loans, 61
Inter vivos, defined, 86
Inter vivos trusts, 65, 68
Intestacy, 47
defined, 86
distribution of assets, 41-42
Intestate, defined, 86
Invalid will, 39, 40, 41-42
IRA, 77
Irrevocable, defined, 86
Irrevocable trust, 52
Issue, defined, 23, 86

Joint ownership, 17, 53
Joint tenancy, 53

Keogh plan, 77

Lapse, 24
defined, 86
Laws, will compliance to, 16
Lawyer
fees, 48
finding right one, 6-7
will safekeeping by, 37
see also Attorney
Legal advice, 6
Legal competence, 39
defined, 86
Life estate, 20
defined, 86
Life insurance, 78
Lifetime trusts, 68
Liquid assets, defined, 86
Living trust, 51-52
defined, 86
Living wills, 82-83
Loans, interest-free, 61

Marital deduction, 58, 67
Minors. *See* Children

Nongrantor trusts, 71-72
No-Nonsense Estate Planning Information Summary, 88

Partnership, 79-80
agreement review, 80
Personal property, defined, 86
Power of attorney, 81

About the Authors

STEPHEN H. GREEN is a Philadelphia, Pennsylvania attorney with degrees from Lafayette College (A.B.), Columbia University Law School (LL.B.) and New York University Law School (LL.M. in Taxation).

PHYLLIS C. KAUFMAN, the originator of the *No-Nonsense Guides*, is a Philadelphia attorney and theatrical producer. A graduate of Brandeis University, she was an editor of the law review at Temple University School of Law. She is listed in *Who's Who in American Law*, *Who's Who of American Women*, *Who's Who in Finance and Industry*, and *Foremost Women of the Twentieth Century*.